Perfectly Ordinary, Yet Extraordinary

Making a Meaningful Difference in the Lives of Others

By Dean and Talya Rotbart

Adapted From "Improbable Lives: A Scot, a Tanzanian,
and Their Canadian Love Story"

Perfectly Ordinary, Yet Extraordinary: Making a Meaningful Difference in the Lives of Others

Copyright © 2020 TJFR Publishing Co, Inc.

All Rights Reserved. No part of this publication may be reproduced, stored in a retrieval system, or transmitted, in any form or by any means, electronic, mechanical, photocopying, recording, or otherwise, without the prior written permission the the publisher.

ISBN – 9781660156498

Library of Congress Control Number: 2019919320

Biography / Ethics / Social Reform

Published by TJFR Publishing Co., Inc.
ATTN: Dean and Talya Rotbart
200 Quebec Street
Bldg. 300, Suite 111-26
Denver, CO 80230

TABLE OF CONTENTS

Introduction	9
"Chapter Eleven:" Making Mrs. Makundi Smile	15
Project Update	39
Lessons Learned	47
Acknowledgements	59
About the Authors	63

Riyaz and Margaret proofreading "Improbable Lives"

Perfectly Ordinary, Yet Extraordinary

Making a Meaningful Difference in the Lives of Others

Introduction

This short nonfiction account is an expanded excerpt from *Improbable Lives: A Scot, A Tanzanian, and Their Canadian Love Story*, scheduled for publication in 2020.

The central characters are Margaret and Riyaz Adat, two perfectly ordinary individuals who have accomplished extraordinary things in the service of others.

Together, they epitomize the ability of anyone – *of everyone, really* – to make a meaningful difference in the world.

Both Margaret and Riyaz immigrated to Canada, a beacon of multicultural tolerance and possibility, in search of better lives and opportunities.

Margaret, one of six daughters of a Glasgow, Scotland, bus driver and a seamstress, was raised in dense government housing, located in an industrial district. Until she was nine years old, Margaret lived in a fourth-floor walk-up, sharing a bed and one of the apartment's two rooms with three of her sisters. The unit had no hot water nor a private bathroom.

Riyaz was raised in Tanzania at a time of significant government upheaval that forced his parents and sister to flee to England without him. Still only a teen, with his family's hard-earned livelihood confiscated, he used his street smarts to survive and ultimately to smuggle himself out of the country at risk of life and limb.

At first, their separate lives in Toronto were challenging. Finding jobs. Navigating a new culture. Making friends. Supplementing their limited education.

Gradually, with hard work and dedication, they each attained professional and personal traction.

Margaret, age 17, was always good with numbers and found a job as an accounting clerk within a month of her arrival in September 1972. Her career ascended steadily, and eventually, as an equity partner, she was responsible for nurturing a bankrupt distributor of high-tech imaging products into one of Canada's *50 Best Managed Companies*.

Riyaz arrived in Canada, via England, in July 1974, age 19. He spent his first two years working as a computer control clerk for a securities firm located in Toronto's financial district. His short-term goal was to earn a professional degree in accounting, and he attended night classes toward that end.

Riyaz needed to earn money not only for himself but also to support his parents and to help fund his younger sister's dental school education. So, when his job with the securities firm plateaued, with no advancement in sight, he went to work as an audit clerk for the City of Toronto. He remained there seven years.

But whether in Tanzania or Toronto, Riyaz was always an entrepreneur at heart, and in 1984 he waved goodbye to the nine-to-five work world and tried his hand at a variety of diverse international ventures, some successful, others less so.

Among his noteworthy wins was his company, Bosaro Biotech, which designed and manufactured a patented, fully adjustable, back care support. The Bosaro line was sold in Canada, the United States, Germany, Japan, Israel, South America, and the Caribbean. For a brief time, 3M, the multinational conglomerate, marketed a sub-licensed version of Bosaro under the 3M brand.

Early in their separate careers, Margaret and Riyaz's paths crossed. Subsequently, at a party in January 1977, they reconnected, and their courtship began. Their marriage in June 1980 should never have gelled. They were raised in radically different religions and cultures, and became a couple when such intermarriages still raised eyebrows.

But where other people see only obstacles, Margaret and Riyaz have always spotted opportunities: In this case, the chance to build a life together, raise a loving family, and make the world a little bit better for those less fortunate than they.

That same "obstacle-to-opportunity" vision is at the core of this writing, because without it, the Adats would never have been able to accomplish so much against such long odds.

For all of their differences in upbringing and life-experience, Margaret and Riyaz share a deeply held gratitude for their many blessings and an inherent desire to give back.

Over the years, generosity flowed from the Adats in multiple streams: quietly helping a friend or neighbor in need; volunteering their time to area non-profit groups, such as Rotary, and – as this book will detail – "adopting" an impoverished school in far-away Arusha, Tanzania, that needed – well – everything, and that with their love and help has rebounded from the precipice to a place where parents jockey to enroll their children.

About This Edition:

It might be an overused bromide, but if Margaret and Riyaz Adat can work philanthropic miracles without great wealth or a formal organization, so can you.

This text aims to inspire others to take up the challenge, be it in a community half-a-world away, or within walking distance.

Margaret and Riyaz asked no one for permission to undertake their efforts to aid the woebegone J.K. Nyerere Primary School. The idea, as you'll read, only struck them as they were enjoying a comfortable vacation safari in the great wildlife parks of the East African nation.

Undoubtedly, others before them – passing the blighted areas along the roadway to the wilderness parks – gave thought to the notion of helping. But thinking, even wishing, is one thing. Doing is altogether another matter.

Improbable as their plan was to help the children at J.K. Nyerere, the Adats made the implausible possible. And so can you.

What Follows:

- **"Chapter 11" – Making Mrs. Makundi Smile:** A reprint, with minor edits and revisions, of a chapter in the soon-to-be-published biography of Margaret and Riyaz Adat, *Improbable Lives: A Scot, A Tanzanian, and Their Canadian Love Story*. This section details the role the Adats played in the resurgence of the J.K. Nyerere Primary School between the years 2007 and 2018.

- **Update:** A progress report based upon the Adats' visit to the school in October 2019.

- **Lesson Learned:** Some thoughts from Margaret and Riyaz, as well as their biographers, Dean and Talya Rotbart, on ways ordinary readers can plan and accomplish their own extraordinary charitable projects.

Riyaz, Mrs. Makundi, and Margaret

"Chapter 11"

MAKING MRS. MAKUNDI SMILE

A man's true wealth hereafter is the good he has done to his fellowmen -
Attributed to various speakers, including Mahatma Gandhi

Howard Back felt like the hereafter was near as he suffered through the severe stomach cramps, nausea, and fever brought on by dysentery.

He'd received the recommended vaccines for typhoid, cholera, yellow fever, and other undesirable illnesses. But dysentery?

"How did people here in rural Tanzania survive?" he wondered, as he pushed some fluid between bouts of vomiting. Nothing like being sick 7,669 miles from home to be humbly reminded of the blessed life he and his wife Laurie Magee-Back enjoy in Toronto. Howard only hoped that he'd recover soon enough to complete his mission and to tell his friends at the Willowdale Rotary Club all about this amazing place.

Thank God that Laurie wasn't ill. And how very fortunate, when it came to accomplishing their goal, that Margaret Adat was on her feet, constructing a plan of action like a general preparing for battle. After all, 700-plus kids and 25 teachers at the J.K. Nyerere Primary School in nearby Arusha were counting on them.

The wheels of this late-August 2015 expedition had been set in motion eight years earlier when Riyaz and Margaret had taken their sons Anil and Seth, both still in college at the time, to Tanzania on a safari. The Adats booked a seven-day expedition with a local tour company. The trip was unforgettable, filled with nature's splendor. "Tanzania is the most beautiful country; it is unbelievable," Margaret exclaimed.

Every day, the Adats stayed in comfortable lodges, and were escorted to the game parks. They explored and returned to their comfortable accommodations at night. Along the route, however, surrounded by the bounty of nature, they also beheld abject poverty. Indeed, while northern Tanzania is home to Kilimanjaro National Park, Serengeti National Park, Arusha National Park, and so many other playgrounds of the gods, it also houses some of the most impoverished ghettos in the country.

Each night, the four Adats would sit around the dinner table and discuss what they'd seen that day, including all the scarcity and hardship.

By Canadian standards, the Adats were by no means wealthy. Perhaps upper-middle-class, if that. Nonetheless, Margaret, Riyaz, Anil, and Seth considered ways they might provide some support, even if not substantial, to the destitute communities that so many other tourists breezed past without so much as a second glance.

An outright donation of cash — at least the amount they could afford — was unlikely to produce so much as a ripple in the ocean of misery they witnessed. No, they needed to leverage their contribution, and they concluded that the best way to do that was through education.

Riyaz and Margaret told David Laizer, the native tour guide and driver who they had hired and come to trust, that they would like to help a local school in some modest way.

"Think about a school and take us there so we can set something up," they requested. From their casual conversations on safari, they learned that David was the father of school-age children, so perhaps his kids' school would be an appropriate recipient?

As the Adats came to understand in the ensuing days, weeks, months, and years, Arusha and all of Tanzania operate according to a different set of rules than those they were accustomed to in Canada, especially as it pertains to philanthropy and their desire to support the education of children in need.

Arusha, with a population of roughly 420,000, is the third-largest city in Tanzania, reliant on a manufacturing and financial services economy that is bolstered by tourism. First settled by the Maasai people in the 1830s, Arusha was conquered and colonized by the Germans in the late 1890s, and then fell under British governance in 1916 during World War I. On Saturday, December 9, 1961, Tanganyika — as it was known at the time — gained its independence as a republic under the leadership of Julius Kambarage Nyerere, an anti-colonial activist and ardent socialist.

Nyerere, often referred to as the Father of the Nation, governed Tanzania from its founding until 1985. Today, the country's largest airport, in Dar es Salaam, as well as numerous government buildings, universities, and roads, are named for Nyerere, including one badly neglected primary school in Arusha that would, years after its construction, occupy a prominent place in the hearts of the Adat family of Sharon, Ontario.

Hand-Me-Downs

In Arusha, residents with money send their children to private schools. Compared with the government-run public schools, these private academies enjoy a higher teacher-to-student ratio, better-paid and trained teachers, and vastly superior facilities. Likewise, the immaculate student uniforms of private school students contrast markedly with the frayed and threadbare hand-me-downs worn by many of the public school children.

Speaking by phone from Tanzania in the fall of 2017, David, the tour guide, recounted that in the 15 years that he has worked — driving visitors along the exact same roads he traveled with the Adats in 2007 — he never before or since has encountered another family like the Adats. No wonder their wish to help the impoverished children of Arusha caught him by total surprise.

By nature, David always took his time to consider his answer whenever an important question was put to him. So, it didn't come as a surprise to Riyaz and Margaret when he told them that he needed to give some thought to their unusual request.

Two days later, David approached the Adats. "I found a school that receives no help," he told them excitedly. David knew the school because he lived only three kilometers, about 1.8 miles, from it. Although the school he recommended was not the one that his children attended, he was acquainted with its headmistress, Mrs. Makundi.

When their safari was over, David obligingly drove the Adats to the J.K. Nyerere Primary School, a grouping of dilapidated structures — featuring corrugated metal roofs and crumbling cement walls — that had the dubious distinction of being the poorest such educational facility in the area, perhaps the country.

Although Riyaz had spent his youth in Tanzania — both in Dar es Salaam

and Shinyanga; and Margaret's Glasgow roots were decidedly struggling blue-collar, nothing had prepared the Adats for the sorry excuse of a schoolhouse that David drove them to, nor for the inspiring effort made by Mrs. Makundi and her team to educate the children in spite of the decrepit, shockingly overcrowded classroom conditions.

The Adats' first clue of what would await them inside was the squeaky, rotting, waist-high brick perimeter wall on which barely clung a rusted remnant of an iron gate. Almost like a wailing siren, it seemed to scream out, "Enter at your own risk."

A beautiful little boy of about six years of age held onto the frame, his eyes wide-open trying to absorb these unexpected visitors.

Before David and the Adats could cross the threshold of that decaying portal and enter the sunbaked, dusty schoolyard, an adult hastily appeared. "*Habari za asubuhi,*" he said excitedly in Swahili, the official national language of Tanzania, and a language that Riyaz has spoken since elementary school. *Good morning.*

One at a time, the teacher took hold and shook David's, Riyaz's, and Margaret's hands, holding his grip longer by far than is the custom in North America. "What can I help you with?" he asked, smiling.

David, translating his conversation into English for Margaret's sake, responded and explained that he brought with him guests from Canada who would like to help the school. Could they please see the headmistress?

Eagerly, the teacher disappeared into the schoolhouse. Although it was still morning, it was already hot and muggy. The Adats were beginning to wilt under the oppressive weather when Mrs. Makundi arrived at the gate.

Instantly, she struck the Adats as a stern, strong, and humorless middle-aged woman. More security guard than headmistress. She wore a bright and colorful African-print cotton dress.

Margaret didn't have to speak Swahili to understand that Mrs. Makundi was less-than-delighted by these foreign interlopers, who'd arrived unannounced. [Such a commanding presence was the headmistress that everyone, everywhere, calls her Mrs. Makundi. Her given first name is Stella, but that fact, undoubtedly, remains unknown to most people.]

Meanwhile, as word spread through the school, other teachers and even some students began to trickle into the schoolyard to see for themselves what was taking place.

Mrs. Makundi recognized David from one or more previous encounters and began to address him in Swahili, unaware that Riyaz could understand every word of their conversation.

"Nothing. They Want Nothing"

"Why would these two people from Canada want to help a school that is off the beaten path of tourists and all but forsaken even by our local government here in Arusha?" she demanded to know. "What do they want in return?"

"Nothing. They want nothing. They just want to help a little," David answered in a futile attempt at reassuring her.

"Well, I don't believe that, everyone wants something. So, what is it?" she insisted. "What do you want," she turned directly to Margaret and Riyaz and asked. "What do they want?" she again pressed David, the heat of her questioning now rivaling that of the morning sun.

"Don't you think the school needs something?" David offered cautiously.

"Of course, we need a lot of things, but I am not letting somebody just walk in," she snarled.

At this point, seeing that this was going nowhere, Riyaz stepped in. "Mrs. Makundi," he began humbly, speaking in perfect Swahili, "you must have a wish that you want for your children to be much happier and better-educated?"

Taken by surprise, she stared at Riyaz, her mouth agape.

Who was this man? He was dark-skinned, but not a black African like her, David, and most of J.K. Nyerere's students. Moreover, he was with a white woman, very white indeed, who clearly didn't understand a word of Swahili.

Riyaz, recognizing an advantage in the element of surprise, pushed. He explained that he had grown up in Tanzania, gone to school in the country, and knew how difficult educating the rural poor could be.

"Would you mind allowing us to contribute something?" he asked. Riyaz's sincere and gentle manner of speech, radiant smile, and kind eyes swayed the headmistress.

"Come in," she relented.

Redefining "Dedicated"

With David and Riyaz sharing the translation duties, Margaret reiterated that their only wish was to help in some small way, perhaps by purchasing books for the children?

"Before you tell me how *you* want to help us, let me take you on a tour," instructed Mrs. Makundi, once more in full control of her emotions and reasoning.

In name only could J.K. Nyerere's assemblage of barracks, bearing leaky and rusted roofs, be called classrooms. There was a total of seven separate sections for seven grades, or "standards" as they're known in Tanzania.

Buckling under the weight of supporting an average of 120 students with only three textbooks to a classroom, Mrs. Makundi's stalwart group of teachers redefined the word "dedicated."

The last time the school had received new books was back in 2001. The teachers had no chalk to write on the faded blackboards. Computers and printers? *No.* Sufficient indoor lighting to illuminate the classrooms during the dark and rainy winter months? *Absolutely not.* Certainly, there must be air-conditioning to offset the sweltering heat that in any given month tops 90 degrees Fahrenheit, with 60% humidity? *Hah!*

Indeed, the lack of indoor lighting meant that all classes had to be conducted strictly during daylight hours, even though on the hottest, most humid days — with no air conditioning — the classrooms more closely resembled group saunas than centers of learning.

Toddlers up to kindergarten started their school day at 7 a.m. and finished at 11 a.m. The rest of the grades attended from noon to 3 p.m.

Three to five "lucky" students squeezed behind desks designed for only

The outside of the J.K. Nyerere Primary School in 2007

two children. The unlucky ones, of which there were many, sat on the moldy floor.

Given the circumstances, the children were amazingly happy and eager. Everywhere she went, they greeted the headmistress with, "Good morning, Mrs. Makundi," or "Good afternoon, Mrs. Makundi."

In Canada or the United States, these classrooms undoubtedly would have been cordoned off with yellow police tape warning: "Danger." "No Trespassing." "Keep Out."

The ceiling paint inside J.K. Nyerere had faded long ago, replaced by dirty water leakage stains and creeping mold that took up residence on every available surface.

In one classroom, a large gap in the roofing exposed rotted wood frames precariously perched above the heads of the students like the sword of Damocles.

Another classroom featured layers of brown calcified paint hanging like badly torn fabric over rows of long wooden benches no wider than kneelers.

Minimum Wages

Not a single window frame was free of missing or broken glass panels; replacing them a luxury for which no funds were available.

On the Adats' first visit, there was no kitchen to prepare meals for the children, because there was no food to serve.

[On the Adats' next visit, the outdoor school "kitchen," as it was called, featured a series of large round pots lifted off the dusty ground by three stones and fueled underneath by low-burning fires. Some variety of gruel filled one round pot to the top. It was covered by a black plastic trash bag held in place by a couple of wooden spatulas, in a futile attempt to keep flies and other insects out. Large leaves covered the other pots.]

Riyaz and Margaret learned that students walked to and from school, many barefoot, from as far away as eight to ten kilometers — the equivalent of five to six miles.

They came from the poorest families in Arusha, primarily farmers, rural workers, and the unemployed destitute. The typical Tanzanian earns under $17,000 CAD annually, $12,750 USD; while domestic workers or cleaners earn $0.90 CAD an hour ($0.68 USD). The teachers at J.K. Nyerere would be delighted to bring home that much; the parents of their students would be blown away by such extravagant compensation.

Tanzania has hundreds of tribes, and the student population at J.K. Nyerere Primary School is a microcosm of the country at large. The children originate from many different clans, each with their own dialect. The predominant tribe at the school is the Masai, whose native language is Maa. But all the students are required to speak Swahili, and they study English.

The majority of the J.K. Nyerere parents would prefer not to send their kids to school at all. Many parents view it as a waste of time and struggle to provide their children the required school uniforms, such as they are. Parents of even the youngest school-age kids would like to keep them on the farm to work the fields and help bring home cash from the crops. It was a constant challenge for Mrs. Makundi and her team to overcome the objections of the parents.

Commonly, Mrs. Makundi explained to the Adats, the children arrive for class hungry. They carry no school supplies and no playful lunch boxes filled with sandwiches, fresh fruit, cookies, and a thermos or juice box. Most children leave school at the end of the day just as hungry, despite an effort to provide them at least a bowl of porridge.

Perhaps, Mrs. Makundi suggested, if the Adats could find their way to institute a reliable food program for the children, it would not only serve as inspiration for the parents to send their kids; it would also facilitate the students' ability to retain more of what they're taught. It is, after all, hard to hear what the teachers are saying when your stomach is growling so loudly.

As much as the school's state of disrepair shocked the Adats, a visit to the bathroom facilities left them aghast.

In a confined space, such as one might expect to find in a Turkish prison, a hole in the mucky cement floor served as the toilet, with two flat stones strategically placed to the left and right indicating where the children were to place their feet. No soap. No toilet paper. A hole punched in the wall provided ventilation, such as it was. And, of course, no running water. An old, dusty, plastic bottle with a yellow handle, half-filled with water, served as a wash station or flushing tank, or both.

Tears filled Riyaz's eyes. He never before realized how lucky he had been to attend private schools in Tanzania.

"How could this be?" he asked.

It turned out that the school received total government funding of $133,900 TZS per quarter, or $81 CAD. That's roughly what North Americans spend for a nice meal for two at a restaurant, a new pair of shoes, a bottle of cologne, or to pay a traffic fine.

In Arusha, Mrs. Makundi had to allocate 30% of the $133,900 TZS for teaching supplies; 30% for "upkeep" of the facilities, such as the maintenance was; 20% for the administration of the school; and 20% to cover the cost of printing the required national examinations for Standards Two, Four, and Seven. Salaries for the teachers were paid directly by the government but hardly amounted to enough to make up for the shortage of on-site housing that other schools routinely provided their faculty.

So, let's do a quick inventory: a crumbling perimeter wall and gate capable neither of keeping students in nor strangers out; leaky roofs; dark classrooms; a lack of textbooks or even chalk; hungry, shoeless children in ratty uniforms; mold everywhere; underpaid teachers, and bathrooms unfit even for hardened criminals.

"That's Your Receipt"

At the end of the tour, Mrs. Makundi took them back to her office. "We need desks," she declared.

Desks?

Why Mrs. Makundi requested desks out of all of the possible donations she might have sought from the Adats is known only to her. Perhaps she thought it most likely this request would go over best with her new Canadian patrons? It was clear, at least at that point in 2011, that offering to feed the children on an ongoing basis was more than the Adats could bite off.

Bathrooms unfit even for prisoners

Margaret and Riyaz looked at each other and wondered. How on earth, both logistically and financially, could they grant Mrs. Makundi's request for desks? The best they could do, they quickly realized, was to give the school a gift of cash and leave it to the staff to arrange to acquire as many desks as their donation would allow.

Now it was Mrs. Makundi's turn to be shocked.

As soon as the Adats handed her the money, Mrs. Makundi called in all the teachers and announced the generous and unexpected donation they'd just received.

"The whole school stopped," Riyaz recalled. Margaret turned to him and said, "That's your receipt." Indeed, the fact that the entire faculty bore witness to the donation ensured that the money would go for desks. Corruption, rampant on the continent, would not extract its share of their donation.

The only request that Margaret and Riyaz made was for the school to send them photos of the desks once they were purchased and delivered. To their delight, the school, with David's assistance, had the desks made locally and provided the Adats the photographic proof that their donation was used exactly as intended.

Service Above Self

For the Adats, their most cherished memory of their first visit to J.K. Nyerere was not the gradual warming of Mrs. Makundi, the appreciation of the faculty, or their well-deserved sense of "mission accomplished."

No, going away, it was the children, a sea of kids in navy-bottom and white-top uniforms who smiled at them, curious and eager to approach, and overjoyed to pause for photos.

Indeed, those smiles reached across the African continent, past the Mediterranean Sea and Atlantic Ocean, around Nova Scotia, and darted along the coast of Lake Ontario, arriving ultimately in the grasp of Howard Back and the four or five other members of the Willowdale Rotary Club who the Adats had gathered to share the tale of their Arusha adventure and their newfound charitable mission.

Among the most famous "residents" of Willowdale, a neighborhood in the Toronto district of North York, is Canadian hockey legend and restaurant namesake, Tim Horton, who was interred in the community's York Cemetery after his death in a single-vehicle crash in 1974, age 44.

Comedian and television host Howie Mandel hails from Willowdale, population 79,500, as does novelist and short story writer Joseph Boyden. Like much of Toronto, Willowdale is a stew of single-family homes, townhouses, and high-rise residential towers. The residents tend to be middle-to upper-middle class, and include a large contingent of Chinese, Korean, and Iranian immigrants.

On Thursdays, the men and women of the Rotary Club of Willowdale, some 30 in all, meet over lunch or dinner to hear speakers, network, and take action to further the mission of Rotary International: providing service to others, promoting integrity, and advancing world understanding, goodwill, and peace.

Rotary's official motto is *"Service Above Self,"* while the annual motto of the International President reads, *"One Profits Most Who Serves Best."*

When Margaret and Riyaz were in Arusha in 2011, they spotted a sign for one of the local Arusha Rotary Club chapters. The sign triggered an idea.

Upon the Adats' return to Canada, Margaret contacted a friend of hers, Sherri Galler, who she knew was involved locally with Rotary. Sherri, in turn, put Margaret in contact with Howard Back, a longtime member and officer of the Willowdale Rotary Club.

The Rotary Club of Willowdale has a distinguished record of public service, dating back to its original charter in 1952. Over the years, members have supported numerous nonprofit projects domestically — such as the planting of trees, and local Salvation Army fundraisers; and far-flung, including the Smiles Foundation, which provides dental care to the children of the Dominican Republic, and a drainage project in the Philippines. Combined, the small, close-knit members of the Willowdale Rotary Club have contributed more than $2.6 million CAD to worthwhile causes.

So, for Margaret to serve as a speaker at a regularly scheduled Rotary weekly luncheon meeting and seek help from those in attendance for a school in far off Tanzania was not as odd as it might otherwise sound.

To help Margaret's chances of winning the club's support, Howard and his wife, Laurie, invited Margaret and Riyaz to their home to meet informally with a few Rotary members. The Backs were accustomed to hosting Rotary gatherings — especially barbecues.

That evening, Margaret shared stories of the inspiring ways that she and Riyaz had been able to make a meaningful difference all on their own. There were the desks they funded. And later came supplies. And even a water tank to bring potable water to the school.

When a colleague of Margaret's mentioned that he was headed to Mt. Kilimanjaro for his honeymoon, Margaret enlisted him to extend his travels by 200 kilometers, or about 124 miles, to drive with his bride to J.K. Nyerere to deliver more cash to Mrs. Makundi.

Never shy when it came to doing good for others, Margaret also found an international shipping company, Kintetsu World Express, that she persuaded to deliver Canadian supplies that the Adats had collected to Arusha, free of charge.

Those gathered in the Back home were impressed - most notably, with Margaret and Riyaz's "just do it" attitude toward altruism. No organizing committees or boards. No fundraising drives. No tax credits. Just giving generously of their time and available resources.

So many other people, similarly situated, would have shrugged off any responsibility for helping, reasoning that their limited financial resources and lack of a formal charitable conduit precluded any meaningful philanthropic impact.

Margaret's two presentations, at the luncheon meeting and in the Back's home, worked. The Willowdale Rotary Club voted unanimously to join with her and Riyaz to expand their efforts on behalf of the school. "Boom," Margaret recalled, clapping her hands with excitement as she reflected on the moment. "They were there to support us."

Through Rotary, Howard and Laurie Back not only became charitable partners with the Adats, but they also became good friends, sharing a common purpose that eventually saw Howard and Laurie, in late August 2015, join Margaret in getting to know the kids and faculty at J.K. Nyerere in person. (Riyaz, who was wrestling with health problems, was unable to make the 2015 trip.)

A former tax manager with KPMG, Howard had operated his own

accounting practice since 1993, helping clients to manage their business finances or build personal portfolios. He took it upon himself to set up and run the financial aspects of Rotary's fundraising for the school.

Back to School

Helping an impoverished school thousands of miles away proved a challenge.

Although there were two or three Rotary Club chapters in Arusha, every attempt Howard or Margaret made to connect with them to coordinate a plan of action was unsuccessful.

Once again, Margaret — now joined by Howard — looked to David Laizer, the tour guide, to help them coordinate their donations and their travel plans, as well as serve as a go-between with the school's headmistress, Mrs. Makundi.

Howard and Laurie had traveled to Europe and the Caribbean together. But nothing prepared the couple for what they were about to encounter in Arusha.

The view from the tiny window of the plane was breathtaking as Margaret and the Backs approached Mt. Kilimanjaro International Airport. Snow-capped, Kilimanjaro towered over the low buildings of the airport, like Gulliver in the land of the Lilliputians. The blue sky, paired with black runways and the yellow-and-green grass of nearby Arusha and Moshi, perfectly evoked the four colors of the Tanzanian flag.

When he isn't suffering from dysentery, Howard, who first joined Rotary in 1980, cuts a figure of a take-charge individual. Five-feet nine-inches tall, with receding chestnut hair and distinguished dark-rimmed glasses, his healthy personality is a mix of humor and energy. Laurie, who married Howard a few years before their journey to Tanzania, is a petite golden strawberry blonde with a ready smile and abundant enthusiasm.

A Few Days in Arusha

In Canada, Margaret and Howard are mere mortals - a business executive and an accountant. However, when they arrived at the J.K. Nyerere school, along with Laurie, the three Canadians were greeted like global rock stars.

Imagine more than 700 squealing children jostling to get a peek at the trio of visitors - and for the lucky ones - a touch. The curious kids, only a few of whom could still vaguely recall Margaret and Riyaz's first visit to the school four years earlier, wanted to feel Margaret's hair, marvel at her blue eyes, and touch her ivory white skin.

Engulfed by swarms of children, Margaret, Laurie, and Howard — as photos of the encounter attest — were wholly at ease, reveling in the adoration of the students and teachers alike.

Their days spent at J.K. Nyerere included some memorable ceremonial exchanges — Canadian flags and lapel pins for each child, and colorful Maasai Shukas, cloth wraps commonly worn by the Maasai people of East Africa, for Margaret, Howard, and Laurie.

Nonetheless, the three visitors quickly got down to business.

An inspection of the school facilities and conversations with Mrs. Makundi and the teachers revealed that conditions — while better in some respects since the Adats' first visit — had worsened in other ways.

All told, the condition of J.K. Nyerere still qualified as abysmal.

Mrs. Makundi, dressed in a bright yellow Maasai Shuka featuring geometric designs, was much warmer to newcomers Howard and Laurie than she had been originally to Margaret and Riyaz.

Over dinner, she told her Canadian benefactors that what the school was still most desperate for — as it had been in 2007 — was decent food to nourish its students. The children were hungry; most received no breakfast at home. Unlike in Canada or the United States, the local and national governments in Tanzania didn't allocate funds to feed students at school.

"Could you provide food for our children?" Mrs. Makundi asked, a hint of pleading in her voice.

What a saintly woman! She obviously loved her children and had dedicated her life to their education and well-being. Now all she was addressing was the basic need to nourish them.

To Margaret, Howard, and Laurie, it was as if Mother Theresa herself was asking for help. And it fell to them to say "no."

The three Canadians were in tears as they explained the reality to Mrs. Makundi. "I am sorry," Howard said, "we can't afford the food to sustain a food program. While we could have enough money to supply food for all the students for maybe one year, what would happen after that? What about the students the next year, and the next? We want to make a more lasting impact on the school, helping not only the current students but many more in future years."

With the funds they brought, along with additional money they felt confident they would yet raise in partnership with the Willowdale Rotary Club, Margaret, Howard, and Laurie knew they could help with much-needed repairs, such as walls, windows, and paint. They could build new washrooms and a wall to protect the school.

But no matter how hard they stretched — both their budget and their imagination — the three patrons couldn't see their way clear to raising enough money to feed the children on a reliable, ongoing basis.

Upon their return to Toronto, Howard and Margaret presented a slideshow to their fellow Rotarians, who warmly embraced the J.K. Nyerere school as a club-wide priority. As a bona fide Rotary project, the Adats were able to expand the appeal to donors, since all contributions would henceforth be tax-deductible, and best of all, none of the donations would be spent on administrative costs.

Obstacles and Mistakes

In the ensuing months, the Adats encountered numerous obstacles and made plenty of mistakes. A shipment of supplies took forever to arrive and cost much more in the end than if they had been purchased in Tanzania.

Funds that the Adats wired were always at risk for being hijacked. One significant money transfer didn't go through because Tanzanian authorities were suspicious that it might be illegally laundered money.

While chasing windmills in Arusha, the Adats also faced challenges domestically, including the illness and subsequent deaths of Riyaz's sister and mother.

Drained emotionally and financially by the medical crises, the Adats gave serious consideration to scrapping their J.K. Nyerere sponsorship entirely.

Mrs. Makundi in yellow, with Margaret, Howard, Laurie, and Emanuel to her left

They didn't.

Eventually, by August 2017, Willowdale Rotary and the Adats were able to raise enough money to cover the cost of meals for two grades of students so that they would be well fed for one month ahead of their crucial national standard exams - the results of which would have a permanent influence on their academic future. Incredibly, 95% of the kids passed.

Fueled by support from Margaret, Riyaz, Howard, Laurie, and the Willowdale Rotary chapter, conditions at the school have shown dramatic improvement over time.

Gone are the moldy Turkish style bathrooms, replaced by a new and functioning washroom building. Fresh paint, both inside and out, adorn fully repaired walls. There are new roofs, floors, and windows. An exterior fence and working gate were added to enhance school security.

Like a proud father, Riyaz boasts that when he and Margaret first started to help J.K. Nyerere, only 20% of the children continued to secondary school. Now the number is approaching 100%.

The total student enrollment at J.K. Nyerere has grown from 700 to 820, an unambiguous sign that parents now see the school as a place they'd like their children to attend.

Amazingly, all this has been accomplished on a shoestring budget. Roughly $82,000 CAD has been raised with the help of the Adats, the Backs, the Rotary Club, and various fundraising initiatives.

Friends and family of the Adats, from as far away as Texas and Scotland, were among those who pitched in, a few hundred dollars at a time. One of Margaret's friends donated the compensation he received for helping out one of her clients.

"Money doesn't play as big a role as we think it does," Riyaz reflects. "It's the motivation; it's caring. It's 'we are in it together. We'll do it; I can do it; you can do it; he will do it.' And that's what makes it happen."

Mrs. Makundi, who since 2001 served as J.K. Nyerere Primary School's dedicated headmistress, has now retired. Emanuel S. Singooy, a Mathematics, English, Geography, and History teacher at the school since 2015, succeeded her.

But Emanuel will be the first to admit that no one can replace Mrs. Makundi.

Margaret recalls that at one point, Mrs. Makundi was struggling personally. Her husband was dying, and her son had quit his job to care for his father. "I gave her some cash and was clear, 'This is not for the school. This is for you,'" Margaret recounts.

It mattered not. Mrs. Makundi shared the funds with J.K. Nyerere.

Julius and Riyaz Side By Side

The irony that Riyaz Adat — whose family in Tanzania enjoyed no special status or political influence — should share the affections of the school and its community with Julius Kambarage Nyerere, the revered national leader for whom the school is named, is not lost on the Adats and those who know of their efforts.

Indeed, on the freshly painted walls of the J.K. Nyerere school hang, in close proximity, a portrait of President Nyerere, and a plaque honoring the Adats and Rotary.

When the Adats rolled up their sleeves and took out their checkbooks to help Mrs. Makundi and her kids, they had no idea that anyone outside of their immediate family and circle of friends would ever take notice.

When they turned to the men and women of the Rotary Club of Willowdale, they did so with only one purpose in mind: to expand their capacity to help.

Yet the Adats, in their modest way, have done much more than help a single, failing school in far off Arusha, Tanzania.

They've demonstrated that the unbridled power of pure hearts, combined with a firm resolve, can indeed change the world, one small corner at a time.

How many of us go about our daily lives feeling helpless, incapable of making a difference?

It's not true.

Like the Adats, we all have the potential to have a positive impact on the lives of those in need.

Education was the ticket out of poverty for Margaret and the map Riyaz followed to achieve a good life for his family and himself.

Only time will tell who and how many of the children at J.K. Nyerere will owe their lifelong good fortune to the efforts of Mrs. Makundi, her colleagues, and the support of the Adats and Rotary.

If the Adats' contributions changed even one life, it was worth it. In all likelihood, eventually, hundreds of graduates of J.K. Nyerere will prove the beneficiaries of Riyaz and Margaret's generosity.

Helping to improve the quality of education and the learning environment of so many school children has and will continue to provide the kids with the keys to a world that most of them never dreamed of entering.

Indeed, the act of giving has ramifications that far outreach a simple act of kindness.

For the children of J.K. Nyerere Primary School, the Adats have helped to provide a portal to a brighter future.

Margaret with a Canadian flag pin for each student

PROJECT UPDATE

Early Christmas morning, 2013, death hovered over Riyaz Adat as he lay in a hospital bed at Toronto General Hospital.

Two days earlier, he marked his 59th birthday, and the odds were overwhelming that it would be his last.

The long, slow march to the edge began back in 1994 when Riyaz was first diagnosed with primary biliary cirrhosis, or PBC, a rare liver disease that, when it does strike, typically afflicts women born in the Northern Hemisphere; making Riyaz's diagnosis all the more unexpected.

"Son, your liver is going to collapse. It's going to go. You have ten to twelve years left," the physician had informed him matter-of-factly.

Her timing, it turned out, was off by almost a decade, but not her prognosis. A gaunt, jaundiced, and rapidly withering Riyaz would be dead before New Year's 2014 if he didn't receive a new liver.

Not that his Christmas Day transplant surgery wasn't grueling, nor his rebound from it agonizing. They were all that and more.

But with his wife Margaret at his side every step of the way, along with his young-adult sons, Anil and Seth, Riyaz postponed his rendezvous with the Angel of Death.

In *Improbable Lives*, the biography of Riyaz and Margaret from which this book is adapted, the chapter detailing Riyaz's harrowing medical journey is titled, "*A Christmas Day Miracle*," which it most certainly was.

But the poignancy of that miracle was never more in evidence than when a healthy Riyaz Adat, accompanied by Margaret, Anil, and Seth, stepped off the plane in Tanzania in October 2019, returning to the J.K. Nyerere Primary School in Arusha to see the progress the school had made since the last time Riyaz was able to visit in 2011.

The eager children, more than 750 of them, who poured out of the school to greet the Adats with fascination and glee, had no clue of just how improbable it was that Riyaz would ever return. Or, to be perfectly honest, that he had ever been there previously.

But fate knew.

It knew that it wasn't Riyaz's destiny to die in 2013. He and Margaret had more work to do in Tanzania, and a failed liver would under no circumstances be allowed to stand in their way.

Called Back

This was Margaret Adat's fourth trip to the J.K. Nyerere Primary School.

For a girl who grew up in the government tenements of Scotland, where the sight of natives of East Africa was a rarity, the prospect of making so many visits to the nation known for its sky-high mountains, lakes, grasslands, and national parks, would have been unimaginable.

Margaret first went with Riyaz and their two sons in 2007. They were there to go on safari, and as detailed in *"Chapter 11,"* only dropped in at J.K. Nyerere on a spontaneous impulse.

She returned again in September 2011, with Riyaz and friends; in September 2015, with Howard and Laurie Back, and in 2019, once again, with Riyaz, Anil, and Seth.

Riyaz returned once in November 2008 with his cousin, Minaz, but without Margaret.

He was too sick to join her in September 2015, so he stayed behind.

This arrival was so markedly different from previous trips, especially the first one, when they met the then-headmaster, Mrs. Makundi.

Though Margaret and Riyaz would never describe themselves as such, this time, they arrived as dignitaries. Many of the faculty faces were fresh, and the children were complete strangers to the Adats.

But the couple from Toronto and their two sons immediately felt they'd come home.

Mrs. Makundi was retired, as were her immediate two successors.
But they all returned to be with the Adats. The new headmaster, Rose Mwaimu, welcomed the Canadians as old friends, even though this was their first meeting.

The transformation of the school infrastructure from the day of the Adats' initial visit in February 2007, was remarkable.

The crumbling, rotting, peeling ceiling, walls, and floors have been replaced or reinforced, looking and functioning like new.

The sorry excuse for washrooms, unfit for prisoners, were long gone. An entirely new washroom building, offering sanitary facilities and privacy, stands in its place.

The collapsing brick perimeter wall with the wailing gate – where the wide-eyed little boy was first to spot the Adats' arrival in 2007 – likewise, is only a memory. Today, the J.K. Nyerere Primary School is surrounded by a protective wall and functional, seven-foot-tall entrance gate.

A modern tank, towering over the schoolyard like Mt. Kilimanjaro looms over Tanzania, provides much needed potable water.

In 2007, Mrs. Makundi asked Margaret and Riyaz for desks for the children, many of whom had to sit on the floor. Today, the children of J.K. Nyerere have proper seating.

The list of improvements goes on and on. School uniforms for all kids, even those with no parent to provide them. *Check.* New supplies. *Check.* A functioning kitchen. *Check.* Electricity in classrooms that had none. *Check.* Meals for students during Standard 4 and Standard 7 national exams, so they don't have to take these crucial tests on an empty stomach. *Check.*

More importantly – actually, *most* importantly – the spirit of the J.K.

Nyerere Primary School is no longer battered and bruised. There is an air of vitality that permeates the campus, a hope, and a belief in a better future, one fueled by education.

The administration of the school prepared formal remarks to greet the Adats on their arrival on October 7, 2019.

The educators' spoken English was not perfect, but their message was unmistakable: The Adats and the Rotary Club of Willowdale have been true guardian angels.

Nonetheless, Margaret and Riyaz are the first to acknowledge that the school remains far from adequate and light-years from the facilities that primary school children in Canada and the United States take for granted.

Even some of the early upgrades that the Adats made with the support of the Willowdale Rotary Club have begun to show the signs of age and wear.

During the welcoming ceremony for the Adats, the administrators shared a wish list for future repairs and upgrades. Among their most pressing needs:

- A computer (imagine a primary school in Canada or America that lacks even one computer) and a photocopy machine.

- A special unit to serve the subset of students at the school with disabilities, especially intellectual impairments.

- Help to provide housing for teachers, who earn meager wages. Unlike many schools in Tanzania, J.K. Nyerere does not offer all of its staff housing.

One intractable problem that Margaret and Riyaz have encountered since their very first visit is that so many of the children arrive at school without having had breakfast, and may have no meaningful meal awaiting them when they return home.

The cost of providing daily meals to hundreds of students remains out of reach for the Adats, the Willowdale Rotary, and any other benefactors who thus far have embraced the school.

Perhaps, one day, feeding all the children will be an achievable goal. Just not yet.

Will Margaret and Riyaz return to Arusha and the J.K. Nyerere school in the future? It's a safe bet that they will. Their hearts are bound to the school and its children, and that's never going to change.

If, dear reader, you will excuse a bit of a fanciful daydream on the part of the authors, it is this:

Not many years from now, Margaret and Riyaz will get a call from a businessman or businesswoman visiting Toronto. The conversation will go something like this:

"Hello?"

"Is this Mrs. Adat?"

"Yes, it is. Who's calling."

"You don't know me by name, but I attended the J.K. Nyerere Primary School. I work for WeFarm as an agricultural engineer in Tanzania. I'm in town on business. I'm hoping to have a chance to meet you and your husband in person and say 'thank you' for all of your support over the years. Without you, I could never have achieved my career success."

Such a call may never come. But it might.

And whether the alumni of J.K. Nyerere Primary School ever recognize the contributions that the Adats have made to their education and careers, matters not.

The Adats' generosity has been repaid many times over in their knowledge that they made a difference in so many young lives. That's thanks enough.

LESSONS LEARNED

There is a well-known proverb: *When the student is ready, the teacher will appear.*

The same is true for homegrown charitable projects: When the leader is ready, the followers will appear.

Many, many people want to do good. They want to make the world a better place. They want to help those in need.

But most people don't have the mindset to launch out on their own and commit to seeing a philanthropic undertaking through to the end.

But you can do it, and this book will help you get started.

The very first lesson is to recognize that when you start out alone on a philanthropic mission, it's only for a while. The purity of your intent and the dedication you demonstrate will attract supporters. Some of them you'll know — including family, friends, colleagues, and neighbors. Others will gravitate toward you, drawn by the prospect of service and feeling good about themselves.

If you build it, they will come.

Margaret and Riyaz began alone with a simple goal: To do something within their means to help the children of the J.K. Nyerere Primary School in Arusha, Tanzania. They had no grandiose designs. Just a nagging acknowledgment that they could do more than turn a blind eye to children in need.

Help Wanted

As they saw how their relatively minor donations began to revive the school — like a teaspoon of water applied to a dried-out sponge — the Adats turned to their local Rotary chapter, hoping to enlist others. It proved to be a smart move.

You may find supporters at similar benevolent social organizations, local religious houses, community centers, amateur sports clubs, or even standing on the street handing out "Help Wanted" flyers seeking like-minded strangers.

Patience is not only a virtue; it's a necessity.

Parenting a charitable project is akin to raising a flesh-and-blood child. It's a role that changes over time, but never really ends.

To succeed, you need a view to the long-term. Yes, if you organize a community car wash or bake sale, it need never be repeated. But those aren't the type of projects we're focused on with this book.

We're talking about making a commitment to the betterment of individuals or institutions that won't be fulfilled in a single day, month, or even a year.

That is not to say that short-term projects aren't beneficial. They are.

It is, however, to ask you to think bigger. Like money that multiplies when funds are invested and reinvested in a savings plan, the effort to make a meaningful difference will be most impactful when you give it the time it requires to compound.

This book showcases the accomplishments of the Adat family in improving the lives of children who attend a distant primary school. It is an undertaking that began in 2007 and is ongoing.

The Adats hope you will be better prepared to launch your own charitable efforts based on their experiences helping the J.K. Nyerere Primary School, just as they were able to apply the lessons they gleaned in Arusha to help the people of Turks and Caicos islands, nearly 7,500 miles from Tanzania.

In September 2017, Hurricane Irma, a Category 5 monster, flattened much of the archipelago of eight major islands located midway between the Dominican Republic and The Bahamas. A tropical tourist mecca, the Adats had vacationed there and befriended a local resident, Kevin.

Hurricane Irma

Kevin and his family were lucky to survive Hurricane Irma, although they and many of their neighbors lost everything they owned except the clothes on their backs. When word of their plight reached the Adats in Toronto, Margaret and Riyaz flew into action.

The J.K. Nyerere Primary School project provided the experience, self-confidence, and some of the connections that saw the Adats collect clothes, shoes, personal items, household goods, books, toys, tools, and even furniture to ship to Turks and Caicos.

In quick order, the Adats built a Facebook page to spread the word of their appeal and to provide updates. They enlisted the help of local businesses and schools, which in turn asked their employees and communities to donate. Some businesses agreed to serve as drop off points for donations, which the Adats collected by the boxful.

Tamara Stokoe-Said, the owner of a Toronto fitness and dance studio, came aboard in a blink. Tamara arranged a Zumba fundraiser with the help of six volunteer instructors. One-hundred percent of the class fees were donated to the Adat project. Many members of Tamara's The MOVE Studio brought bags and boxes of donated items as well.

Another local business, Max Brakes, served as a drop-off for donations and also stored the items. In addition, the company bought several skids of new small kitchen appliances — such as blenders and toasters — to ship to Turks and Caicos.

Thanksgiving 2017 was especially memorable for the Adats, as they spent much of the day sorting and packing donated items in their garage.

Of course, the biggest challenge was how to get all the donated items from frosty Toronto to balmy Turks and Caicos, where so many people had been left to sleep under the stars.

Margaret turned to Donato Atoni, a friend who is the president of a freight forwarding company, Kintetsu World Express (Canada), based

Satellite photo of Hurricane Irma, taken September 10, 2017. (Credit: NOAA/NASA)

in Mississauga, Ontario, seeking a quote on transporting a large cargo container to Turks and Caicos. She and Riyaz expected to drain a lot of the cash donations they'd received to pay for the shipping costs.

But generosity is infectious. And Donato, upon learning of their mission, waived all fees, delivering a 40-foot container, filled to the brim, to those in desperate need. Donato and his wife also wrote the Adats a personal check to help out.

Kevin, the Adats' friend in Turks and Caicos, reported back that Margaret and Riyaz's efforts helped more than 1,000 people in the island territory, mostly Haitians. There is a large community of Haitians in Turks and Caicos, most of them there without the proper papers. The Haitians did not want to go to government help centers for fear that they would be deported.

The Adats pay no heed to the race, nationality, or religion of those in Turks and Caicos, Arusha, Toronto, or anywhere. As Riyaz explains, "We're all living in this one world, so if we can help in some way, that gives us great pleasure."

What follows are specific insights that Margaret and Riyaz have gleaned from their self-directed philanthropic efforts. They are intended to ease the way for others who will undertake their own charity projects.

Trust

Until the Rotary Club of Willowdale embraced Margaret and Riyaz's efforts in Arusha, the Adats had no formal organization to vouch for the sincerity of their efforts, and no method to allow donors to deduct their contributions for tax purposes.

They were one couple asking for support of a distressed primary school 7,669 miles away, with little more than their word to offer as substantiation.

Would you donate to them if they approached you?

Happily, many people did, because they knew Margaret and Riyaz, and their word was good enough.

When you first seek the help of others, be it monetary or in the form of services and endorsements, the trust you've fostered over the years will serve as a goodwill bank, from which you'll readily be able to make "withdrawals."

Most obviously, the first people to approach are family members and friends, as well as those you know through work, both vendors and customers.

Not only do you have history with these contacts, but they know "where you live" — and they know that you're not going anywhere anytime soon, having absconded with their donations.

A penny that doubles to two cents on day one, four cents on day two, eight cents on day three, and so on, will surpass a million dollars on day 27.

Trust is like that.

You reach out to those who already trust you. They reach out to those who trust them. And so on and so on.

Soon, you have an extensive network of donors and supporters who'll help without all the formalities of a name-brand charity.

Cashless

The hardest "ask" in the charity universe is for cash.

In support of a good cause, or in response to a request from someone they know and trust, many people are willing to donate items, services, or their time far more readily than they are to write a check.

To build momentum for your project, it's often wise to begin by asking for favors — not money.

Among those to whom Margaret and Riyaz first turned for non-monetary assistance, a large percentage eventually also donated cash to their J.K. Nyerere project.

Moreover, getting a second or third donation from the same people became quite common in the Adats' experience, as their donors formed a connection to the cause and felt good about themselves each time they contributed.

Naysayers

Brace yourself.

> *Your proposal is impractical.*
>
> People won't support you.
>
> *Your efforts won't make any difference.*
>
> There are worthier causes.

Yup! There are more reasons than you can possibly imagine that non-doers will assure you that you are doomed to absolute failure. Your project will go down in flames, and you with it.

Most critics believe what they're saying, even if subconsciously, they are threatened by your actions in the face of their inactions.

We don't advise dismissing their dire warnings out of hand. You should know where the obstacles might lie and the mines may be buried. Listen for those truths in the negativism flooding your way, and then make a plan to navigate past the impediments.

Let the facts in but not the emotions.

You must remain confident in your purpose and your ability to achieve your goals. Setbacks are inevitable. Often, the thin line between success and failure comes down to believing fully in yourself and your mission.

Permit no one, no matter how well-intentioned or accomplished they are, to plant the seeds of doubt in you.

One final note on this point. Margaret and Riyaz discovered that some people never put their money where their mouth is. That is, some people promised the Adats they'd be generous supporters, but never followed through.

In business, Margaret Adat is not one to be trifled with. Make Margaret an empty business promise or fail to pay a debt, and you'll hear from her.

When it comes to the J.K. Nyerere project, however, Margaret and Riyaz elected to be, well, more charitable.

After all, the Adats reason, donations must genuinely come from the heart. At least they'd like them to. Thus, pressing someone who does not give freely seems to them to be overstepping the charitable spirit of their efforts.

Each charitable organizer must decide for himself or herself just how hard to pursue collections.

You're Only Human

When Riyaz's health declined precipitously in 2015, Margaret had only one priority - Riyaz. He didn't have the strength or focus to continue his efforts on behalf of the J.K. Nyerere school, and Margaret didn't have the bandwidth to spend time or attention on their charitable project.

So they didn't.

Life happens, for better or worse.

Weddings need to be planned, babies are born, jobs are lost (or started), relocations take place, you name it. A host of realities can interfere with the best of charitable plans and intentions.

So be it.

Ideally, as the Adats did, you can find a co-pilot who'll be able to carry forward when you need to take a break from your philanthropic efforts. In the case of Margaret and Riyaz, fellow Rotarian Howard Back and his wife Laurie stepped up when Margaret was tending to Riyaz.

Recently, life events have required the Backs to take a pause, so Margaret and Riyaz have again become the point-persons on the project.

Although it seems improbable that Margaret and Riyaz will ever walk away from J.K. Nyerere permanently, they do recognize that self-directed charities needn't last a lifetime.

In fact, if you need a momentary hiatus or a permanent break, the Adats say the only valid perspective for doers is to measure what they have accomplished against what would have been achieved if they had not acted in the first place. Everything greater than zero is a victory.

The same goes for those periods of life when no major obstacles stand in the way, yet doers find themselves regretting all the undone tasks on their to-do lists.

As they reflect on the lessons of their J.K. Nyerere project, Margaret and Riyaz begin to list all that they might have done — and still have to do. In this respect, they've not yet fully internalized their own advice.

Enough is never enough in the eyes of the charitable doer. But it has to suffice. More than that, "enough" has to drown out any thoughts of inadequacy or insufficiency. They are counterproductive.

Eventually, the Adats hope that the J.K. Nyerere Primary School will become self-sufficient, able to meet the needs of the children, faculty, and facilities without their help or that of other international donors.

Other charities, such as those dedicated to fighting poverty and hunger, are — realistically — never going to achieve obsolescence.

As Robert Kennedy is quoted as saying: "Every generation inherits a world it never made; and, as it does so, it automatically becomes the trustee of the world for those who come after."

The charitable doers of tomorrow stand on the shoulders of those making the effort now. The examples set by Margaret, Riyaz, and other like-minded self-starters are the foundation stones of a better tomorrow.

Commitment & Generosity

As exceptional as Margaret and Riyaz Adat have been in their charitable pursuits, they are — as the title of this book notes — also perfectly ordinary.

In closing, the authors of this text want to share three brief examples of similar self-directed charitable efforts in which they had a hand. We believe these projects reflect the type of commitment and generosity embodied by the Adats.

Two women in frosty Denver, Colorado, who wanted to do something to help the poor and homeless cope with the brutal winters. They began a drive to collect socks to distribute through shelters and related non-profits.

The first year was a trickle. But their selfless efforts attracted the attention of Dean Rotbart, who was co-hosting a local, weekly, broadcast radio program. Dean invited the women on his show and spontaneously came up with the concept of asking Denverites to go sockless one day a year and use that day to donate new socks to the cause.

Thus, *No Socks to Work Day* was created, with no funds or institutional backers. The idea quickly caught on and spread as area businesses, churches, and schools began their own sock drives. Even the mayor of Denver, Michael B. Hancock, showed up at City Hall, sockless, as did the coach and some of the star players of the city's National Basketball Association team, the Denver Nuggets.

Within six weeks, thousands of pairs of socks had been donated and copycat drives were launched in other states.

Ryan McFarland is a successful entrepreneur in Rapid City, South Dakota. He loves the outdoors, bikes, and kids. To help his first child, Bode, learn to bike at a young age, Ryan tooled a no-pedal balance bicycle in his home garage that allowed Bode to propel himself using his legs and learn how to balance on a bike, even before his son's leg muscles were sufficiently developed to power pedals.

Ryan's invention, the Strider Balance Bike, evolved into a global phenomenon, with toddlers as young as 18-months biking alongside their parents and older siblings. Ryan's company has sold millions of the bikes.

But Ryan was concerned about kids who never have the opportunity to learn to bike, and instead pass their days sitting indoors in front of their digital screens. To his way of thinking, biking should be as fundamental as reading, writing, and arithmetic.

So with other like-minded South Dakotans, Ryan formed a non-profit organization, The Strider Education Foundation, to provide free bikes and a proprietary "Learn to Ride" curriculum to primary schools for the benefit of their kindergarten-age students.

When Ryan reached out to Dean Rotbart, who had done communications consulting for Ryan's company in the past, Ryan's goal was to expand the bike donations program significantly.

Together, Ryan and Dean created the nationwide All Kids Bike® movement, a grassroots fundraising drive with an audacious goal: Teach every child in America how to ride a bike before they reach first grade.

Like the Adats and the two Denver sock campaign organizers, the All Kids Bike® campaign — which is ongoing — began to attract donors and supporters as word spread of Ryan's mission. A growing number of "National Ambassadors" have lent their names and full endorsement to the campaign, which has spread to more than 150 schools across 27 states, and counting.

Long before Talya and Dean Rotbart met Margaret and Riyaz Adat, they faced a similar dilemma. The Rotbarts wanted to contribute to the local Jewish day school where their children were enrolled. But unlike the mega-donors who wrote big checks and had classrooms or entire building named for them, Talya and Dean didn't have those kinds of funds available.

So they asked themselves, "How can we leverage the dollars that we have available to donate?"

They turned to Eran Grebler, a second-generation Israeli ceramicist, who handcrafts dreidels, the spinning tops that are central to the festivities of the Hanukkah holiday. Grebler's dreidels are functional works of art that buyers from around the world display not just during the official eight-day holiday, but year-round.

Talya and Dean used their entire donation pool of funds to buy a wide variety of Grebler's ceramic dreidels - some elegant, others playful. They donated the dreidels to their children's school and just before Hanukkah helped market them to the entire Denver Jewish community.

Because the Rotbarts bought in bulk, they were able to acquire the spinning tops at below-retail prices. Moreover, they emphasized in their marketing materials that 100% of the proceeds from each sale would go directly to the school, with no amount held back for the cost of acquiring the dreidels or running the sale.

In the end, Talya and Dean were able to quadruple the dollars they donated compared with their original, available funds.

In every community in Canada and America, there are undoubtedly dozens of other self-directed doers who've acted, without any official authority or backing, just because they heeded the call of those in need.

We hope this book inspires you. We hope it sparks some ideas of ways in which you can contribute to improve the lives of others. We hope it provides you with some practical means to push your projects forward and learn from the mistakes that Margaret and Riyaz made.

The Final Secret

Here's the final 'secret' of being perfectly ordinary yet extraordinary: Giving generously of yourself means you're anything but ordinary. You are phenomenal. God bless you.

Christmas 2018

ACKNOWLEDGEMENTS

Although *"Perfectly Ordinary, Yet Extraordinary"* is focused on the Adats and the independent manner in which they helped the J.K. Nyerere school, the title aptly applies to many others mentioned, and unmentioned, in this book who likewise have found a way – their own way – to contribute to the school, its children, its families, and its community.

Margaret and Riyaz wish to recognize and extend their appreciation to:

- Their immediate family, Anil, Seth, and Sandra Adat
- Chris Abrahamse
- Hilary & Hafeez Ali
- Gulshan Alibhai
- Donato Atoni
- Laurie & Howard Back
- Minaz Bata
- Shanaz Bata
- Ave & Randi Bradford
- Nicola Buckley
- Tom Berend & Michelle Strom
- Joan & Sharon Caddie
- Canadian Imaging Trade Association
- Cantrex Nationwide Group
- Christine Clark
- Pamela Copari
- Victoria Copari

- Aniz & Zahir Dhanani
- Rosie Dias
- Julie Ferlisi
- Bill Fortnum
- Sherri Galler
- Elizabeth Galic
- Nazim Gilani
- Erin Goldberg
- Scott Hull
- Kintetsu World Express (Canada)
- P. J. Kursell
- David Laizer
- Claudia & Harry Mac
- Dr. Richard D. Mackenzie
- Gerardo Magno
- Stella Makundi
- Tracey McGlynn
- Kevin Moore
- Lynne Moore
- Arzina Murji
- Brenda Nadel
- Bhoke Nyerere
- Anabela Pacheco
- Debbie & Richard Pinto
- Talya, Dean, Maxwell & Avital Rotbart
- Mina Shah & Arvind Varma
- Rose Sinclair
- Emmanuelle Singooy
- Bashir Somani
- Keri Vos
- Estate of Nan Wallace
- Michelle Wallace
- Gina Wang
- The Whitmer Trudel Charitable Foundation
- Ashley Yang
- And many others

MAY WE ADD YOUR NAME TO THE LIST?

One-hundred present of the revenues from the sale of this book, after expenses, will be directed toward the children of the J.K. Nyerere Primary School in Arusha.

But we hope you'll also consider making a stand-alone donation on behalf of the children. Depending upon where you live, your contribution may be tax-deductible. Please consult your tax advisor.

To join with Margaret, Riyaz, and the many other generous supporters, please visit the Rotary Club of Willowdale website at: *willowdalerotary.org*.

About the Authors

Dean and Talya Rotbart are the authors of the forthcoming book, "*Improbable Lives: A Scot, A Tanzanian, and Their Canadian Love Story,*" a biography of Margaret and Riyaz Adat.

Dean is a Pulitzer Prize-nominated former reporter and columnist with *The Wall Street Journal*. Since 2012, he has served as host and executive producer of *Monday Morning Radio*, a weekly small business podcast.

He also is chairman and editor-in-chief of the *Business News Luminary Awards,* which recognize outstanding achievement by journalists.

Talya writes children's books and is a romance novelist. She is a talented vocalist and painter.

The couple lives in Denver, Colorado. They have two adult children, Maxwell and Avital, who like their parents, are published authors.

Made in the USA
Monee, IL
27 January 2020